Beverages

Cookies & Bars

Other Yummy Desserts

Spiced Apple CIDER

serves 8

INGREDIENTS

64 fl. oz apple cider
1 Tbsp   brown sugar
          orange zest
          cinnamon sticks
          whole cloves

DIRECTIONS

Place apple cider and sugar in a large pot over medium heat.
Stir until sugar dissolves.
Add orange zest, cinnamon sticks and cloves to cider mixture.
Bring cider to a boil, then reduce heat and simmer for 20 minutes.
Pour cider through a strainer into a large punch bowl.
Garnish mugs with cinnamon sticks and cloves.
ENJOY

Spiced Cider by Molly Wilson from Rockledge, FL (mollykwilson.com)

peperminty hot

① 1 1/2 c. heavy cream

② 6 oz. bittersweet chocolate chopped

chocolate

+ 1 1/2 c. milk

+ 1/4 c. sugar

+ 1/8 tsp salt

combine + med. low heat and steam

+ 3 drops peppermint oil

+

③ garnish with sweetened whipped cream and chocolate shavings!

Rudolph's cinnamon mango frappé

ingredients:
- 2 cups frozen mango chunks
- 1/2 cup plain or vanilla yogurt
- 1 tbsp each of:
  milk
  sugar or honey
- 1 tsp each of:
  cinnamon
  vanilla
  lemon juice
- 1/8 tsp nutmeg

★optional:
(for extra flying power)
- 1 or 2 scoops vanilla protein powder

Combine all ingredients
(except mango) & blend with
a hand blender or mixer. Add mango
a few at a time & blend until smooth.
Enjoy with a spoon or add
more milk for a creamy drink.
Partially freeze for a chillier dessert.

Serves 3 (1 cup servings)
(make extra batches to share
with boss & 8 tiny friends.)

© Angela Matteson

Rudolph's Cinnamon Mango Frappe by Angela Matteson from Columbus, OH (angelamatteson.com)

CHRISTMAS TEA with vanilla pod

Christmas Tea With Vanilla Pod by Patrycja Lapatiq from Torun, Poland (www.patrycjawrobel.pl)   9

Warming wintery
CO_COA
DRINK

1 tablespoon cocoa powder

sugar
milk (2 cups)
water (1 cup)

1 cinnamon stick

6 dried cloves

dark chocolate

6 pods of cardamom

Warming Wintery Cocoa Drink by Kristina Alijosiute from Vilnius, Lithuania (behance.net/kristinaa)

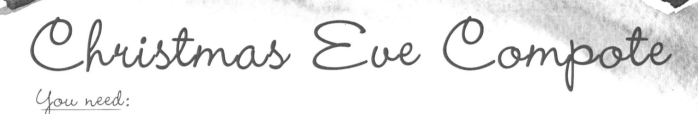

Christmas Eve Compote

You need:

 28 oz. of dried fruits (apricots, apples, plums)

 1 little lemon

 2 spoons of honey

 5 cloves

How to do it:

1. Peel the lemon zest.
2. Put dried fruits into a pot & cover with warm water. Leave for few hours (to let fruits soften).
3. Add cloves, lemon zest and 3 quarts of water.
4. Boil the compote about 30 minutes (low fire).
5. Then add the honey.
6. Serve warm or chilled.

THE HOLIDAY COOKIE

SaNTa'S (SECRET) RECIPE:

- Mix Sugar, Oil & Eggs in Bowl
- Sift Flour, Baking Soda & Baking Powder in Bowl
- Mix BOTH BOWLS, along With BUTTERMILK, Salt & Vanilla & Mix Well! Then, Place 1/4 cup of the Batter per COOKIE on ungreased Baking Sheets.
- Sprinkle With Sugar, Sprinkles, cinnamon & Bake for 10 Minutes in 400° Oven or until Lightly Browned.

ENJOY!

1 1/2 cups Sugar • 1 cup veg. oil • 2 eggs • 3 cups flour • 1 TS baking Soda • 1 TBS baking Powder

1 CUP BUTTERMILK • 3/4 TS. SALT • 3/4 TS VANILLA EXT. • 5 TBS CINNAMON

The Holiday Cookie by Abz Hakim from Toronto, Canada (abzhakim.blogspot.com)   15

BaNaNa OATMEAL CookiEs

ingredients:

3 medium ripe bananas, mashed
1/3 c butter, melted
2 c uncooked quick-cooking gluten-free oats
1/4 c skim milk
1/2 c cranberries
1/2 c walnuts
1 tsp vanilla extract

1. Heat oven to 350°F.
2. Mix all ingredients together in a bowl.
3. Let batter stand for about five minutes, then drop heaping teaspoons of dough onto a greased cookie sheet.
4. Bake for approximately 15-20 minutes or until cookies are lightly browned. Remove to wire rack to cool.

Makes about 2 1/2 dozen cookies.

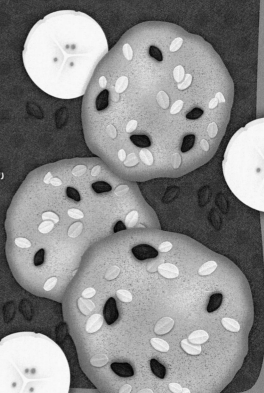

sugar-free
gluten-free
egg-free

Stained Glass Window Cookies

★ hard candies
★ 4 ounces (1 stick) butter
★ ¼ cup sugar
★ 1 ½ cups flour
★ 1 tbsp milk

Mix butter & sugar, then add flour & milk

Roll out to approx 5mm thick

Cut out circles then cut a shape in the centre

18

bake for 15-20 mins, make sure sweets have set hard before removing from tray

place on baking tray with a sweet in each cookie hole

Add another hole when cookies are warm and you can hang them on your Christmas tree!

©Sarah Ward 2010

Stained Glass Window Cookies by Sarah Ward from Sheffield, UK (gingerbred.co.uk)   19

Florentines

Bejewelled biscuits sparkle in the Christmas firelight and are a lovely present for mums!

Ingredients

(makes 15)

2 oz butter
2 oz natural brown sugar
2 oz corn syrup
2 oz plain flour

1 oz glacé cherries
1 oz candied angelica
2 oz candied peel
2 oz flaked almonds
3-4 oz chocolate

Melt the butter, sugar and syrup over a low heat. Off the stove add the chopped peel, cherries, angelica, almonds and finally the flour.

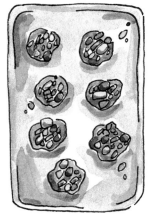

Put teaspoonfuls of the mixture on lined baking trays and bake at 350°F for 8-10 minutes until golden brown.

Reshape with a knife and let cool until they are stiff.

Melt chocolate and spread on the backs. Leave to set.

Merry x x x Christmas x Mummy.

RUSSIAN TEA CAKES

INGREDIENTS

1 cup butter
1 teaspoon vanilla extract
6 tablespoons powdered sugar
2 cups all-purpose flour
1 cup chopped walnuts
1/3 cup confectioners' sugar for decoration

DIRECTIONS

Preheat oven to 350 degrees

In a medium bowl,
cream butter and vanilla until smooth.

In a separate bowl, combine 6 tablespoons
of powdered sugar and flour.

Add the sugar/flour mixture
to the creamed butter/vanilla
and stir until the dough holds together.
Mix in chopped walnuts until evenly distributed.

Roll dough into 1 inch balls and
place on an ungreased cookie sheet about 1 inch apart.

Bake for 12 minutes.

Once cooled, roll cookies in 1/3rd cup powdered sugar.
Roll again for an extra snowy looking cookie.

Russian Tea Cakes by Laura Mayes from Ann Arbor, MI (lauramayes.com)   23

1 and 3/4 cup Flour

1 teaspoon Vanilla

3/4 cup SUGAR

three room temperature EGGS

2 teaspoons baking powder

1/2 cup of butter melted & cooled

24

in a LARGE mixing bowl, beat EGGS & SUGAR. Add cooled Butter and vanilla. Sift in flour & baking powder.

let pizzelle iron pre-heat ---------- use spoon to DROP BATTER onto Pizzelle IRON. Check pizzelles after 45 seconds, leave in iron until desired BROWN color.

pizzelles

sprinkle with POWDERED SUGAR!

Pizzelles by Kristin Nohe from Bel Air, MD (knohe.blogspot.com)   25

YETI APPROVED

Gingerbread
COOKIES

INGREDIENTS:

8 OZS
UNSALTED BUTTER

1 CUP DARK
BROWN SUGAR

3 TSP
CINNAMON & GINGER

1 TSP
CLOVES

TWO
LARGE EGGS

1 CUP
MOLASSES

6¼ CUPS
ALL-PURPOSE FLOUR

1 TSP
SALT

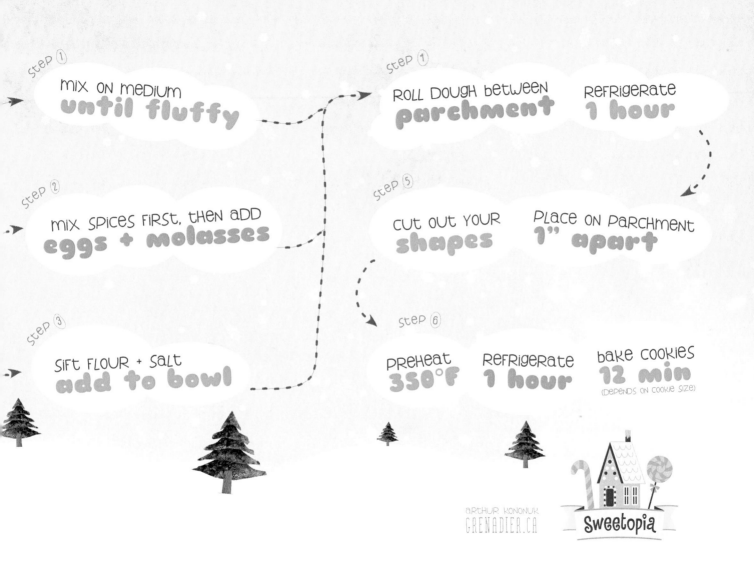

STEP ① MIX ON MEDIUM **until fluffy**

STEP ② MIX SPICES FIRST, THEN ADD **eggs + molasses**

STEP ③ SIFT FLOUR + SALT **add to bowl**

STEP ④ ROLL DOUGH BETWEEN **parchment** REFRIGERATE **1 hour**

STEP ⑤ CUT OUT YOUR **shapes** PLACE ON PARCHMENT **1" apart**

STEP ⑥ PREHEAT **350°F** REFRIGERATE **1 hour** bake cookies **12 min** (DEPENDS ON COOKIE SIZE)

ARTHUR KONONUK GRENADIER.CA

sweetopia

Yeti Approved Gingerbread Cookies by Arthur Kononuk from Ontario, Canada (sweetopia.net)

Yule Log Cookies

NUMM NUMM Tasty

Ingredients

1 egg
3/4 cup Sugar
1 teaspoon Salt
3/4 Cup Soft butter
1/2 teaspoon Vanilla
2 cups flour

Ingredients for topping

1 tablespoon Shortening
2-6 oz. Chocolate Chips
1 cup festive Sprinkles

...Timber!

Bring Some Joy to your World!

Heat oven to 350°

Combine butter, sugar, vanilla and egg.

Shape dough in 2 inch logs on ungreased cookie sheet.

Bake 12 -14 minutes until light brown. Cool.

Melt chocolate chips with shortening.

Dip both ends of cookie in chocolate, then sprinkles.

Place on wax paper.

Enjoy!

Yule Log Cookies by Kaitlyn McCane from Philadelphia, PA (kaitlynmccane.com)

HEALTHY HOLIDAY GINGER COOKIES

2¼ C. white whole wheat flour, 2 t. ground ginger, 3/4 t. ground cinnamon, 1/2 t. ground cloves, 3/4 C. sugar, 1 t. baking soda, 1/4 C. unsweetened applesauce, 1/2 C. canola oil, 1/4 C. molasses, 1 large egg

1 Preheat oven to 350°F. Combine flour, sugar, spices and soda; set aside.

2 Beat together applesauce, oil, molasses and egg. Stir dry ingredients into the mixture to form a dough.

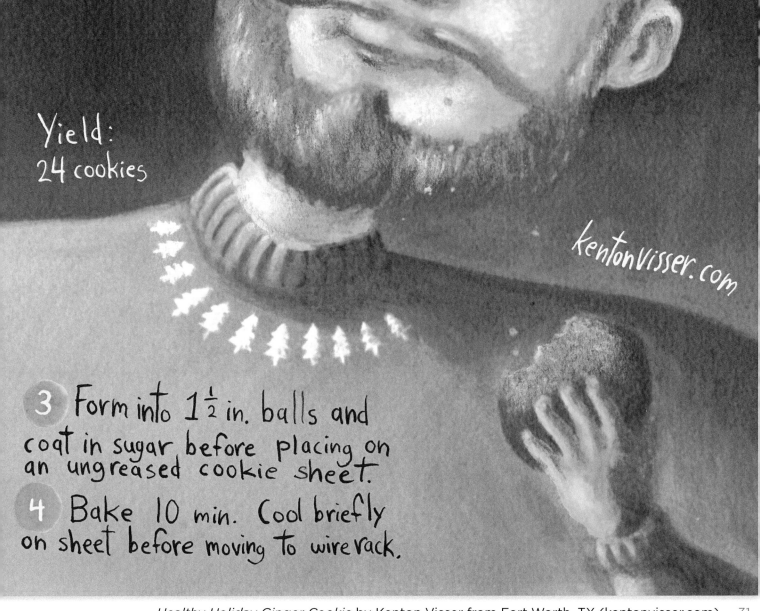

Yield:
24 cookies

kentonvisser.com

3 Form into $1\frac{1}{2}$ in. balls and coat in sugar before placing on an ungreased cookie sheet.

4 Bake 10 min. Cool briefly on sheet before moving to wire rack.

Preheat oven to 400°.
Combine butter and sugar.
Add the egg and vanilla extract
and beat until creamy.
Gradually mix the flour and
baking powder into the buttery
mixture. Using a cookie press,
push the dough through onto
an ungreased cookie sheet.
Add colored sprinkles. Move
cookies into oven and bake for
7 to 8 minutes. Cool. Serve.

1.5 cups of butter
1 cup of sugar
1 egg
1 teaspoon of vanilla extract
4 cups of all-purpose flour
1 teaspoon baking powder
Colored sugar sprinkles

Spritz by Branden Vondrak from Cleveland, OH (brandenvondrak.com)   33

1/2 CUP
HONEY

1/2 CUP
CHOCOLATE
CHIPS

1/2 CUP
PEANUT BUTTER

1/2 CUP
OATS

1/2 CUP
UNSWEETENED
FLAKED COCONUT

1 1/2 CUP
DRIED FIGS &
DATES

1/2 CUP
PUMPKIN
SEEDS

1/2 CUP
ALMONDS

FESTIVE
COCONUT
NUTTY BARS

Place figs and dates in a food processor and pulse until size resembles rice. Add all other ingredients and pulse until mixture sticks together. Press firmly into an 8x8 inch baking pan. Cover tightly with plastic wrap and refrigerate for 30 minutes before cutting into squares. Store in airtight container in refrigerator.

Christmas tree Cookies

preheat oven to 350°

8 ounces softened butter
1/2 cup brown sugar
1 egg yolk
2 cups flour
2 teaspoons cinnamon
pinch of salt

For the icing:
1 egg white, lightly beaten,
2 cups of icing sugar,
cake decoration

baking parchment
plastic wrap
cookie cutters
rolling pin
coloured ribbons
large straw

1 mix butter and sugar
until creamy
then add the egg yolk and mix

2 sift flour, salt and
cinnamon into mixture
and stir until combined

3 shape dough into 2 balls,
wrap them in plastic wrap
and chill them in the
refrigerator for about 30 minutes

4 roll out the dough

stamp out cookies and stamp out rounds
in the top of each shape, using a straw

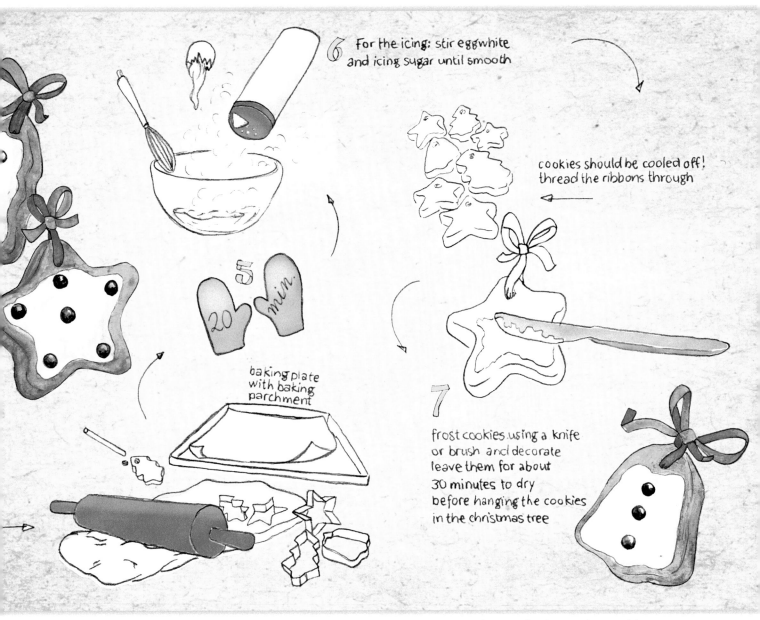

6 For the icing: stir eggwhite and icing sugar until smooth

cookies should be cooled off! thread the ribbons through

25 min.

baking plate with baking parchment

7

frost cookies using a knife or brush and decorate leave them for about 30 minutes to dry before hanging the cookies in the christmas tree

MAPLE
Snickerdoodles

The perfect chewy cookie to swap
with friends or leave out for Santa.

2 CUPS
all-purpose flour

1½ TSP
baking powder

¼ TSP
baking soda

1½ TSP
cinnamon

½ CUP
butter

1 CUP
white sugar

1 egg

¼ CUP
maple sugar

½ CUP
white sugar

¼ CUP
maple syrup

350°

Preheat oven to 350°F.

Combine dry and wet ingredients.

Combine flour, baking powder, baking soda, and cinnamon.

In a separate small bowl, combine remaining white sugar and maple sugar.

In a separate bowl, cream together butter and sugar.

Roll dough into 1" balls and then roll in sugar mixture.

Add egg and maple syrup to creamed mixture and beat until combined.

Place balls 2" apart on baking sheet and bake for 8-10 minutes or until golden brown.

marisaseguin.com

Maple Snickerdoodles by Marisa Seguin from Vancouver, Canada (marisaseguin.com)   39

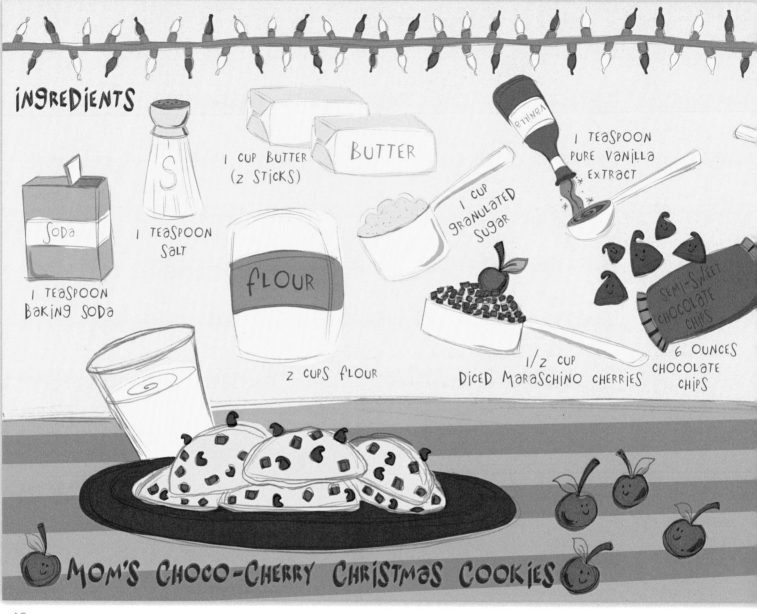

INGREDIENTS

1 TEASPOON
BAKING SODA

1 TEASPOON
SALT

1 CUP BUTTER
(2 STICKS)

BUTTER

2 CUPS FLOUR

1 CUP
GRANULATED
SUGAR

1 TEASPOON
PURE VANILLA
EXTRACT

1/2 CUP
DICED MARASCHINO CHERRIES

6 OUNCES
CHOCOLATE
CHIPS

SEMI-SWEET CHOCOLATE CHIPS

MOM'S CHOCO-CHERRY CHRISTMAS COOKIES

DIRECTIONS

1. IN MIXING BOWL, COMBINE SOFTEN BUTTER AND SUGAR, BEAT UNTIL CREAMY.

2. BLEND IN VANILLA EXTRACT.

3. COMBINE FLOUR, SALT AND BAKING SODA.

4. ADD DRY MIXTURE TO CREAMED BUTTER AND SUGAR UNTIL DOUGH FORMS.

5. GENTLY STIR IN CHOCOLATE CHIPS AND DICED MARASCHINO CHERRIES.

6. STIR IN (OPTIONAL) NUTS.

7. DROP BY ROUNDED TEASPOONS ONTO UNGREASED COOKIE SHEETS.

8. BAKE AT 375 DEGREES FOR 10 TO 12 MINUTES OR UNTIL COOKIES ARE A LIGHT GOLDEN BROWN COLOR.

9. ALLOW TO FULLY COOL, THEN PLACE IN A FUN WAX-PAPERED TIN TO SHARE WITH FAMILY AND FRIENDS OVER THE HOLIDAYS!

(OPTIONAL)

1/2 CUP CHOPPED NUTS

Mom's Choco-Cherry Christmas Cookies by Sandee Chamberlain from Atlanta, GA (sandeescribbles.com) 41

santa is vegetarian
and trying to
lose a few...
maybe 10-15

Vegan Spice Cookies

1 1/2 c + 1 TBS flour
1 1/4 tsp ground ginger
1 tsp cinnamon
1/4 tsp ground cloves
1/4 tsp nutmeg
1 TBS cocoa powder
1/2 c vegan margarine
1/2 c brown sugar
1/4 c molasses
1 tsp baking soda
(dissolved in 1 1/2 tsp boiling water)
1/4 c sugar

whisk together:
flour, ginger, cinnamon, cloves,
nutmeg + cocoa in small bowl. set aside.
-beat together margarine + brown sugar. add molasses + mix.
-add 1/2 the flour mixture + combine well.
-add the rest of the flour mixture.
-chill covered for at least 1 hour. preheat oven to 325 degrees.
-spoon dough into 1 1/2" balls + roll in sugar
-bake 13-15 minutes, until surface starts to crack slightly.

mr. reindeer is vegan, of course.
he is drinking soy hot cocoa with
a vegan marshmallow...yes there
is such a thing!

Vegan Spice Cookies by Salli Swindell from Hudson, OH (studiosss.tumblr.com) 43

MIX in a bowl:
½ cup sugar
1 cup butter
1½ cups flour

PRESS into a
9×9 inch buttered pan.
Poke holes in the top.

BAKE at 350°F
for 20-30 minutes.

Shortbread by Paula Pertile from Sacramento, CA (paulapertile.com) 45

Tipsy Holiday Oranges

In saucepan combine:
2C sugar, 2C water, 2C dry white wine, 12 cloves,
2 cinnamon sticks.
Cook, stir constantly til sugar dissolves.
Simmer 15 more min. Remove from heat.
Add 1 tsp. vanilla.
Cut rind & white membrane from 10 large navel
oranges. Pour syrup over oranges. Cover and
refrigerate overnight. Makes 10 servings

Tipsy Holiday Oranges by Jane Pakis from Chicago, IL   47

Maple–
Topped

1/2 cup
orange juice

1/2 cup
fresh or frozen
cranberries

3/4 cup
low-fat frozen
vanilla yogurt

1/2 teaspoon
finely shredded
orange peel

1/4 cup
dried cranberries

1 1/2 tablespoons
pure maple syrup

Cranberry Frozen Yogurt

Combine fresh or frozen cranberries, orange juice and dried cranberries in a medium saucepan. Bring to a boil over high heat.

Reduce heat simmer uncovered 7 to 8 minutes or until cranberries pop and sauce thickens slightly.

Remove from heat stir in syrup.

Serve warm, at room temperature, or chilled over frozen yogurt. Garnish with orange peel.

Maple-Cranberry Frozen Yogurt by Wirin Chaowana from Nonthaburi, Thailand (wix.com/vc_stang/wirin)

Traditional British MINCE PIES

Santa's favourite work-time treat

Don't forget the carrot for Rudolph!

FOR THIS RECIPE YOU WILL NEED: 12oz SHORTCRUST PASTRY, 1 JAR OF MINCEMEAT. 1 TBSp MILK, A 12-HOLE BUN-TIN (PLUS BUTTER TO GREASE), A PASTRY BRUSH & ROUND CUTTERS

1. Pre-heat the oven to 200°C/380°F.
2. Lightly grease the bun-tin.
3. Flour your surface and roll out the pastry to around 4mm thick.
4. Cut out 12 large and 12 medium circles. Press the large circles into the tin and fill each one with a spoonful of mincemeat.
5. Brush the edges of each pie with milk and press on the lids. Seal the edges with a fork and press a hole into each lid. Brush the top of each pie with milk.
6. Bake in the oven for 15-20 minutes until golden-brown.
7. Serve warm with a dusting of icing sugar and brandy butter.

Traditional British Mince Pies by Hannah Brown from West Midlands, UK (hannah-f-b.blogspot.com)

forest spice cake

1 1/2 cups flour
1 cup oatmeal
1 cup brown sugar
1 cup granulated sugar
1 1/2 tsp soda
1 tsp cinnamon
1/2 tsp salt
1/2 tsp nutmeg

1/2 cup shortening
1 cup water
2 eggs
2 tbls molasses
1 tsp vanilla
1 cup chopped walnuts
1 cup raisins

Heat oven t0 350˙. Grease and flour baking pan.
Measure all ingrediants in large mixer bowl. Mix
1/2 min on low speed. Beat 3 min on high speed .
Pour into pan.
Bake 35 to 40 min, or until wooden pick
comes out clean. Cool and remove from pan.
Cool cake completely before adding rum
syrup.

*Decorate with a rum glaze topped with nuts.

TO:

FROM:

rum syrup

Prepare a light syrup using 1 cup of white sugar and 1/4 cup of water. Heat over medium heat. Add 1 tbs of butter and stir until completely melted. Remove from heat and let cool. Add rum to taste. Prick top and sides of cake with a toothpick. Brush on syrup and let it soak into the cake. * Cake becomes very moist so be careful when moving it to the serving plate.

Forest Spice Cake with Rum Syrup by Wilma Sanchez from Bedford Hills, NY (racoonillustration.com)   53

Perfect dessert for Christmas ☆

Vanilla icecream

Strawberries Balsamico sauce

4 TABLESPOONS BALSAMIC VINEGAR

1-2 TEASPOONS BROWN SUGAR

Instructions:

- heat the vinegar and add sugar
- stir until the liquid caramelises

Vanilla Ice Cream w/Strawberries in Balsamico Sauce by Irena Inumaru from London, UK (irena-inumaru.com)   55

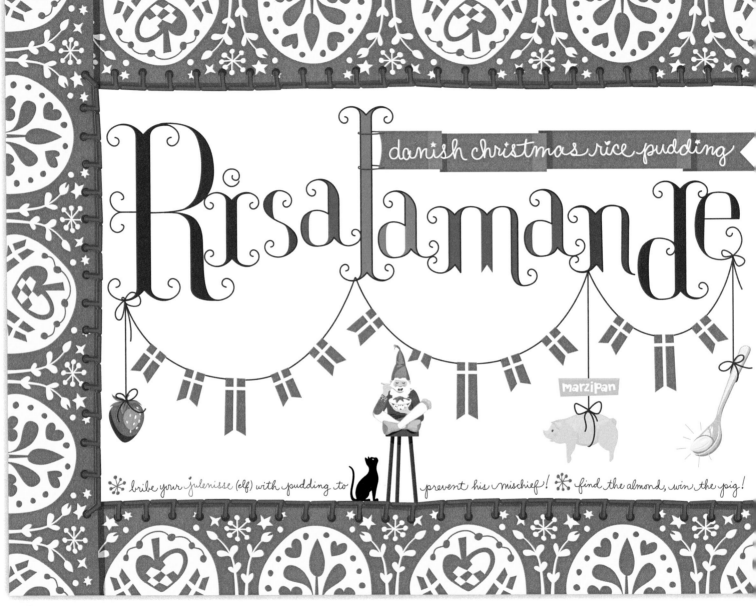

Risalamande

danish christmas rice pudding

✳ bribe your julenisse (elf) with pudding to prevent his mischief! ✳ find the almond, win the pig!

marzipan

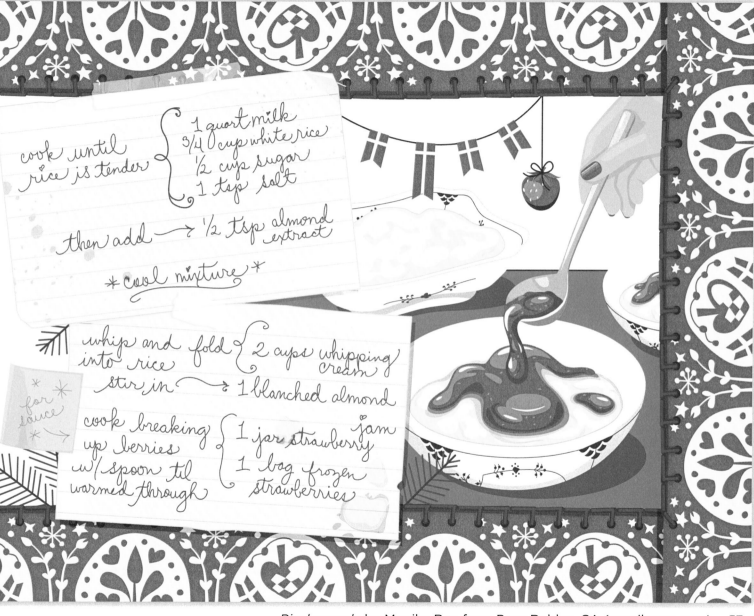

cook until
rice is tender ⎰ 1 quart milk
           ⎱ 3/4 cup white rice
             ½ cup sugar
             1 tsp salt

then add → ½ tsp almond
              extract

* cool mixture *

whip and fold ⎰ 2 cups whipping
into rice   ⎱   cream

stir in → 1 blanched almond

* for sauce *

cook breaking ⎰ 1 jar strawberry jam
up berries   ⎱ 1 bag frozen
w/ spoon til   strawberries
warmed through

Risalamande by Monika Roe from Paso Robles, CA (monikaroe.com)   57

1/2 POUND SUGAR

+

30 + 4× EGGS

MIX WITH →

= YUMMERS!!

1/4 + 1/4 POUND FLOUR

+ 1/4 TEASPOON BICARB-SODA

+ 1/2 TEASPOON MIXED SPICES

POUND BREADCRUMBS

WRAP EVERYTHING IN PARCHMENT + FOIL AND

STEAM FOR 4 HOURS

AND AGAIN FOR 2 HRS BEFORE SERVING

Peppermint Ice Cream Sandwiches

A scoop of Peppermint Ice Cream + **Two Chocolate Chip Cookies** = Yum!

Ice Cream Sandwiches by Tamara Henderson from Atlanta, GA (tamarahendersonstudio.blogspot.com)

* matcha refers to finely-milled Japanese green tea.

Put all ingredients except cherries in a blender and blend at HIGH for 2 minutes.
Stir in ½ bottle of cherries, coarsely chopped.
Pour into lightly oiled cake pan and bake at 170°C/325°F for 40~50 min.

matcha Cheesecake

ingredients: pinch salt
cream cheese, 250 grams (8 oz.)
heavy cream, 200 cc (4/5 cup)
fresh eggs, 3
flour, 3 Tablespoons
sugar, 100 grams (2/3 cup)
matcha powder, 2 Tablespoons
maraschino
cherries,
1 sm. bottle

Chill
thoroughly.
Garnish
with
remaining
cherries
before
serving.

Matcha Cheesecake by Deborah Davidson from Sapporo, Japan (etegamibydosankodebbie.blogspot.com)   63

HOLIDAY COFFEE CAKE

kUgElHOpf

(koo • ghel • HOff)

64

INGREDIENTS

1 PACKET YEAST • 1/4 CUP WATER • 1 TSP SALT
2 TBSP SUGAR • 1 CUP GOLDEN RAISINS • 1 TSP VANILLA
3/4 CUP SLIVERED ALMONDS • 1 GRATED LEMON • 2 BEATEN EGGS
1/2 CUP MELTED BUTTER • 2 CUPS WARM MILK • CONFECTIONERS SUGAR

DIRECTIONS

- ADD YEAST TO LUKEWARM WATER. ADD SUGAR AND LET STAND FOR 1/2 HR IN WARM PLACE.

- MIX FLOUR, 1 CUP SUGAR, RAISINS, SLIVERED ALMONDS, VANILLA, SALT, LEMON RIND.

- CREATE WELL IN THE MIXTURE FOR THE YEAST, MIX + STIR.

- STIR IN 2 BEATEN EGGS, MELTED BUTTER + MILK to MAKE SMOOTH DOUGH. SPRINKLE WITH FLOUR + LET RISE IN WARM PLACE. (2 HRS OR MORE)

- PUNCH DOWN DOUGH + SHAPE INTO RING IN A GREASED 10 INCH TUBE PAN. COVER WITH DAMP TOWEL + LET RISE 1 HR.

- BAKE AT 325° FOR 1 HR.

- SPRINKLE WITH CONFECTIONERS SUGAR + LET STAND OVERNIGHT.

ENJOY!

mix Sugar, salt, flour
add ½ butter, yeast,
water, eggs

knead dough dipping hands
in the other ½ of butter

NUTS EGGS
SUGAR HONEY
& CINNAMON
BUTTER milk   mix and warm
                 in

• ROLL DOUGH until thin !
• Spread filling & roll
• place ongreased pan
  brush with beaten egg
• let rise for 30 mins
• BAKE for 1 hour at 350°

POTICA "excellent pastry"

ingredients:

10 cups flour
3/4 cups sugar
1 teaspoon salt
1 pint warm milk
3/4 cup butter
3 packages dry yeast
1/2 cup warm water
3 well beaten eggs
2 pounds ground nuts
2 cups sugar
3/4 cups honey
13 ounce can condensed milk
1 teaspoon cinnamon
3/4 cup butter
3 eggs well beaten

Christmas
Pav Lova

ingredients
-> -> ->

* 1 tablespoon Corn flour
* 6 egg whites
* 1 teaspoon Cream of tartar
* 1 ⅓ cups caster Sugar

* 1 teaspoon Vanilla extract
* 1 teaspoon White vinegar
* 1 cup pure cream
* Strawberries
* passionfruit

Method

Step 1
- Preheat oven to 400°F
- Draw a 25cm (diameter) circle on a sheet of baking paper
- Dust lightly w/ corn flour

25cm

25cm

Step 2
- Using an electric mixer, beat eggwhites & cream of tartar in a large bowl until soft peaks form
- Add sugar 1 tablespoon at a time, beating constantly until thick & glossy
- Add remaining 3 teaspoons of cornflour w/ the last spoon of sugar. **Then** fold through Vanilla & Vinegar

MIX

Sugar

Vanilla

Step 3
- Spoon meringue onto baking paper
- Shape into a circle, using the pencil mark as a guide
- Make sure the edges are higher than the centre
- Reduce oven to 200°F & bake for 1¼ hrs or until dry & crisp
- open oven door & leave in oven to cool

Step 4
- place pavlova onto plate
- Spread w/ whipped cream
- decorate w/ strawberries & kiwi fruit

fruit

Delicious

Snowy Apple

Ingredients for one

2 cinnamon biscuits

1 greek yogurt

1 apple

Snowy Apple by Sara Zampedri from Ivrea, Italy (sarazampedri.tumblr.com) 71

Holiday GRAHAM CRACKER COTTAGE

INGREDIENTS
6 graham crackers

1 box of powdered sugar

3 Tblsp. meringue powder

Assortment of Candy

FROSTING:
In a bowl, mix sugar, meringue powder and 6 Tblsp. of water. Place one cup of frosting in a plastic bag. Snip the corner of the bag, squeeze out frosting.

*Note-

Build the cottage with 4 crackers for sides and 2 crackers for roof.

Use the frosting to attach the sides, roof and candies. HAVE FUN!

*meringue powder is made from egg whites.

Make a Village!

Holiday Graham Cracker Cottage by Sharon Mann from Las Vegas, NV (sharonmanndesigns.com)

Chocolate Strawberry Tart

1 cup crushed almonds

30 butter cookies

2 tbsp sugar

1 egg white

1 cup heavy cream

3 tbsp butter

9 oz semisweet chocolate

25 oz strawberries

Preheat the oven to 350°F. Beat together the broken cookies, nuts, egg white, and sugar until fine crumbs form. Press them over the bottom and up sides of a tart pan. Freeze for 10 minutes. Cover the crust with foil and bake for 20 minutes. Remove the foil and bake for 5 more minutes.

Meanwhile, heat the cream and butter until butter melts. Remove from the heat, add grated chocolate and let stand to melt. Whisk until smooth. Let stand about 1 hour until cool. Pour into the crust. Place strawberries on the filling. Refrigerate for 2 hours for the filling to set.

Chocolate Strawberry Tart by Nata Metlukh from San Francisco, CA (notofagus.com)

apricots drenched in Chocolate &

- (12 oz. dried apricots)
- melt 1 TBS. butter + 16 oz. bag of semi-sweet chocolate chips in double boiler
- dredge each apricot through chocolate then dip into shallow bowl of ground almonds (coating both sides)
- place on parchment lined baking sheet and place in fridge for 15 minutes to set chocolate

(eat remainder of warmed chocolate with a big spoon + a big smile)

DUSTED with almonds

Apricots Drenched in Chocolate & Dusted w/Almonds by Salli Swindell from Hudson, OH (studiosss.tumblr.com)

meringues

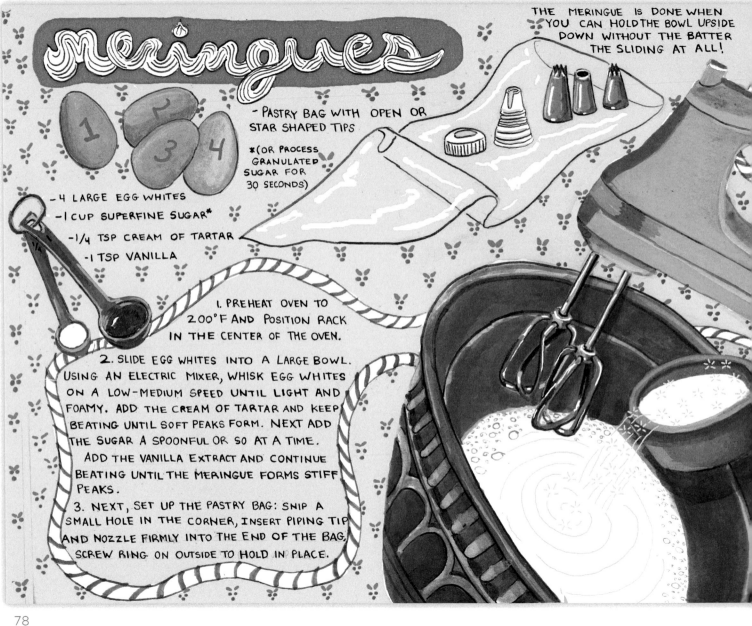

THE MERINGUE IS DONE WHEN YOU CAN HOLD THE BOWL UPSIDE DOWN WITHOUT THE BATTER THE SLIDING AT ALL!

- PASTRY BAG WITH OPEN OR STAR SHAPED TIPS

*(OR PROCESS GRANULATED SUGAR FOR 30 SECONDS)

- 4 LARGE EGG WHITES
- 1 CUP SUPERFINE SUGAR*
- 1/4 TSP CREAM OF TARTAR
- 1 TSP VANILLA

1. PREHEAT OVEN TO 200°F AND POSITION RACK IN THE CENTER OF THE OVEN.

2. SLIDE EGG WHITES INTO A LARGE BOWL. USING AN ELECTRIC MIXER, WHISK EGG WHITES ON A LOW-MEDIUM SPEED UNTIL LIGHT AND FOAMY. ADD THE CREAM OF TARTAR AND KEEP BEATING UNTIL SOFT PEAKS FORM. NEXT ADD THE SUGAR A SPOONFUL OR SO AT A TIME.

ADD THE VANILLA EXTRACT AND CONTINUE BEATING UNTIL THE MERINGUE FORMS STIFF PEAKS.

3. NEXT, SET UP THE PASTRY BAG: SNIP A SMALL HOLE IN THE CORNER, INSERT PIPING TIP AND NOZZLE FIRMLY INTO THE END OF THE BAG. SCREW RING ON OUTSIDE TO HOLD IN PLACE.

4. Using a spatula, scoop some of the meringue batter into the bag only fill the bag 2/3 full. Use your fingers to squeegee batter twist top of bag and hold with one hand while placing other hand by nozzle to guide bag.
*Use a dollop of meringue in each corner of parchment paper to adhere to baking sheet.

Squeeze from the top hand so you don't form air bubbles.

5. Pipe rounds of meringues in rows onto baking sheet.

6. Bake the meringues for 1½ hours or until they have a firm shell and can be peeled off the sheet in one piece. Turn off oven and leave open a crack for several hours allowing the meringues to dry out. Serve with fresh fruit or ice cream!

Meringues by Jessica Pollak from Providence, RI (firstpancakestudio.com)   79

1 **smash**

2 **melt**

3 **add**

4 **spread**

5 **break**

(after cooling in fridge)

6 **melt, dip**

parchment paper

for an extra treat sprinkle bark bits on ice cream, cupcakes or in your hot chocolate!

©2010, Monika Roe

A very special thanks to all the wonderfully talented illustrators whose recipe artwork appears in this book:

Kristina Alijosiute, Erika Barriga, Julianna Brion, Hannah Brown, Sandee Chamberlain, Wirin Chaowana, Deborah Davidson, Abz Hakim, James Gulliver Hancock, Tamara Henderson, Irena Inumaru, Koosje Koene, Arthur Kononuk, Patrycja Lapatiq, Sharon Mann, Kristeen Martin, Angela Matteson, Laura Mayes, Kaitlyn McCane, Amy McKay, Nata Metlukh, Deborah Mori, Kristin Nohe, Jane Pakis, Paula Pertile, Jessica Pollak, Monika Roe, Wilma Sanchez, Marisa Seguin, Monika Sommer-Lapajew, Adam James Turnbull, Kenton Visser, Branden Vondrak, Sarah Ward, Molly Wilson, Meta Wraber and Sara Zampedri

THEY DRAW & COOK™

Designed & edited by Nate Padavick and Salli S. Swindell
studiosss.tumblr.com

Produced & published by They Draw & Cook
Studio SSS, LLC
13 Steepleview Drive
Hudson, Ohio 44236
theydrawandcook.com